YOUNG PEOPLE OF THE BIBLE

A DRINK OF WATER

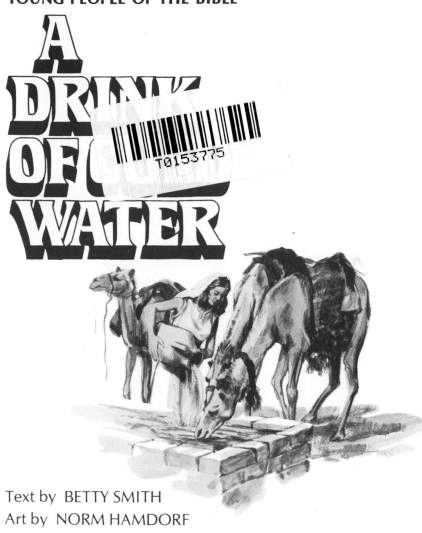

Text by BETTY SMITH
Art by NORM HAMDORF

LUTTERWORTH PRESS
GUILDFORD AND LONDON

First British Edition 1980
Copyright © 1978 Lutheran Publishing House, Adelaide.
Printed in Hong Kong

Ten camels plodded across the bare, hard earth. The afternoon sun threw tall shadows on the ground, but the man on the leading camel still shaded his eyes from the glare. He was very tired, and hoped the end of his long journey was at hand.

Wait! Was that a palm tree away over there? Perhaps he just thought he saw it. He closed his eyes, and felt them sting with the dust and heat. When he opened them again — yes, it was still there! The town was in sight at last.

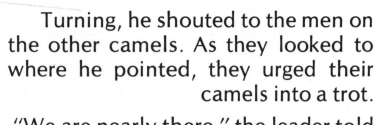

Turning, he shouted to the men on the other camels. As they looked to where he pointed, they urged their camels into a trot.

"We are nearly there," the leader told them. "Only a little while longer and there will be food and water for us all."

The camels grunted as their pace quickened. They could feel how excited their riders were, and instinct told them water was near. They moved faster still, and all the little bells on their harness jingled and rang.

"We are nearly there," they seemed to sing. "Nearly there, nearly there."

It was almost evening when the train
of camels reached the city gate. The
leader gave the watchman his name
and his reason for coming. Then quietly
he guided the camels through the
traffic of people and animals to the

well at the edge of the town. He ordered his camel to kneel down, and slid from its back. With a sigh of relief, he stretched his tired body. The other riders did the same.

"Shall we water the camels?" they asked, for all of them were servants, even the man in charge.

"No, not yet."

The others were surprised.

"It will soon be dark," they reminded him.

Still he shook his head.

"No, we'll wait for a while."

They leant against their kneeling camels, watching and waiting. It was toward evening, the time when the women came to draw water from the well. The leader watched the women as they came out from the town; when they made no attempt to speak to him, he looked away again.

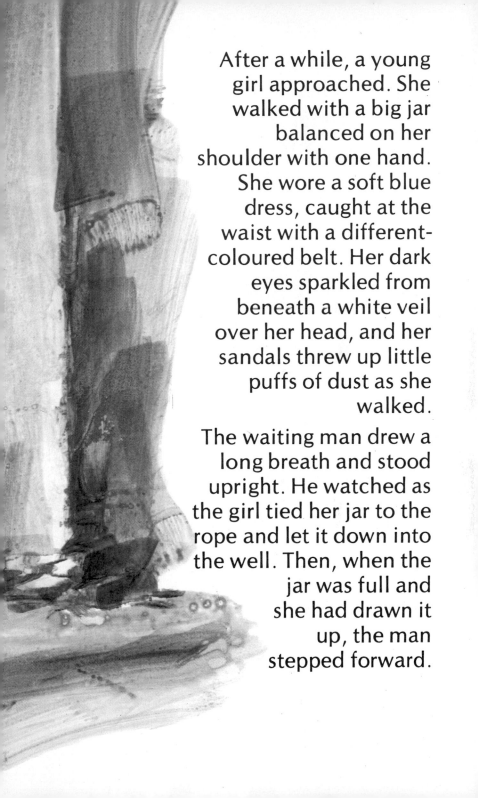

After a while, a young girl approached. She walked with a big jar balanced on her shoulder with one hand. She wore a soft blue dress, caught at the waist with a different-coloured belt. Her dark eyes sparkled from beneath a white veil over her head, and her sandals threw up little puffs of dust as she walked.

The waiting man drew a long breath and stood upright. He watched as the girl tied her jar to the rope and let it down into the well. Then, when the jar was full and she had drawn it up, the man stepped forward.

"Will you give me a drink, please?"
She smiled at him.
"Yes, certainly."
Lifting the jar, she held it with both
hands so that he could drink. As he

drank, she saw the line of waiting camels, with their riders beside them.

"Have you come a long way?" she asked. "Your camels must be tired and thirsty, too. I'll draw more water for them and for your friends."

The man looked at her in silent surprise. For a moment she wondered why, but forgot about it as she used her jar to fill the big stone trough for the camels.

"Come and drink, and bring your camels to the trough," she told the men. Again and again she filled her jar, and kept pouring the water into the trough until both the thirsty men and their camels had had enough.

The leader stood watching the girl as she hurried about her work, but he said nothing until she had finished. Then he spoke quietly, "We need somewhere to stay tonight. Is there room in your father's house?"

She was surprised, but answered pleasantly, "My father is dead;

my brother Laban is the head
of our house. My name is
Rebecca. We have
enough room and food
for all, but I'll go
and ask."

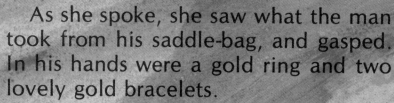

As she spoke, she saw what the man took from his saddle-bag, and gasped. In his hands were a gold ring and two lovely gold bracelets.

"These are for you," he said.

She could hardly believe it!

"For me? Oh, but . . ."

"I'll tell you all about it when I see

your mother and brother," the man said. "Don't be afraid to take these presents. Soon you'll know why I've come to this town."

Rebecca didn't quite know what to do. At last she said, "Wait here!" and hurried away.

Her home was nearby, and she ran in, calling, "Mother! Laban!"

Her mother and brother came running to her. Rebecca hurriedly told her story and showed the presents.

"There's something strange about this," said Laban. "I'll go and bring the men here. In any case, they'll want a meal."

Soon the tired travellers were sitting in Rebecca's home. They had washed away the dust of the journey. Hay and water had been left in the stable for the camels. When the women were about to serve the meal, the leader said, "Before we eat, I must tell you my story."

"Very well," said Laban, "we'll wait and listen."

"Do you remember your great-uncle Abraham?" the man began. "He lives in the land of Canaan. God has made him a rich man, and everyone respects him. He owns many sheep and cattle and camels, and I am his chief servant."

"My husband often wondered what happened to his uncle," said Rebecca's mother. "I'm glad to know Abraham is still alive, and has done so well for himself."

"He has one son at home — Isaac," said Abraham's servant, "And now Isaac is old enough to marry. My master doesn't want him to choose a girl from Canaan, for the people there worship idols. So he decided to send me here to find a girl from among his own people to be Isaac's wife."

"But this is the wonderful part," the man continued. "I didn't know how I could find the right girl, for there would be so many in the town. How could I know which one would be right for Isaac? So I prayed to God."

"Did He answer you?" asked Laban.

"Yes, indeed He did. You see, I asked Him to guide me by a sign. If a young woman at the well not only gave me a drink, but at the same time offered to give water to all my camels, too — well, I'd know that she was the one God has chosen for Isaac."

"Why, that's just what I did!" said Rebecca.

The man smiled.

"Yes, I know. Then, when you told me who your people were, I knew that God had led me to my master's relatives."

He stood up and bowed. "Will you come back with me?" he asked.

For a while Rebecca didn't answer.

Then she said shyly, "Yes, I will go. God has chosen me. If I trust Him, I'll be doing the right thing."

So, soon after, Rebecca rode away to become the wife of a man she had never seen before. Today, this seems a strange thing to do, but it was part of God's plan for that family. Isaac loved his young bride dearly. In time, there were twin baby boys to make their father and mother proud and happy. As the boys grew older, they must have heard over and over again the story of what happened when their mother gave someone a drink of cold water.

Something to Remember: When Jesus our Saviour was on earth, He reminded us that even giving a cup of water to someone in need is just the same as helping Him. Because Rebecca loved God, she thought of others beside herself, and was happy to help them. God is pleased when we love and help others because we love Him.

A Verse to Learn: "Love one another as I have loved you." (John 15:12)